What Really Goes on in the Workplace

By: Sharon Ford

Published by

Ford-Mill Publishers
Austell, Georgia

10 9 8 7 6 5 4 3 2 1

First Edition © 2016 by Sharon Ford

ISBN 978-0997556711
Illustrated by Ford-Mill Publishers
Cover Design by Victoria Valentine Designs
Photographer: Dawn Nelson
Printed in the United States of America
Library of Congress Control Number 2016945919

DEDICATION

THIS BOOK IS DEDICATED TO MY ONE AND ONLY SAVIOR, JESUS CHRIST. THANK YOU FOR RELEASING ME TO WRITE THIS BOOK AND BELIEVING IN ME WHEN NO ONE ELSE DID. I WILL ALWAYS LOVE YOU. *SHARON*

CONTENTS

INTRODUCTION

Throughout our everyday lives and in the back of some minds, we often wonder: What other job may be dealing with the same drama as mine? Well, let me tell you, the people may change, but the storyline remains the same.

It doesn't matter about race or gender, drama is still drama. Some people tend to take their work or work-related problems home with them. As for me, well, let's just say as soon as I clock out, that drama is left behind except for the memories.

Sometimes, the work environment can be stressful and funny at the same time. Throughout the different types of jobs I've had, I sometimes wonder why God kept me at these places. Now I know it was to share these stories with the world to let them know nothing is hidden that shall not be revealed.

One of these incidents may be happening in your place of work even as you are reading this book. Just in case you have the type of job where you've never seen some of this stuff go on, and everybody gets along, and it's just peaches and cream, well, my hat goes off to you and your company and maybe you can teach a seminar on how the rest of the world can be like you. Until then, read, enjoy, and pray.

1

THE STRIP CLUB

Your workplace is simply where you get your source of income. We all have seen the movie The Players Club. Well, I'm not taking away from the movie, but being an ex-stripper, it didn't nearly scratch the surface about what really goes on. I started stripping when I was 20 in 1990 until 1995.

My cousin, who was a stripper at the time, used to show me how much money she used to make taking off her clothes. One day, she took me down to meet one of the managers; it was around lunchtime so not a lot of people were in the club. When I walked in, I saw women on stage naked, and the music was pumping.

After speaking with the manager, he had me turn around and then the nerves kicked in. He said, "Take off your clothes. I need to see what kind of shape you're in."

Everyone had to go through this screening process because not only did you have to pay a certain amount a night, which was $35 to the manager on shift and tip the D.J. but they needed to make sure that they could make money off you. If you couldn't make money, then how were you supposed to pay them to dance in the club?

My first day, I was so nervous because I started right then. The day crowd was much nicer than the night crew, so I started there first. I didn't worry about my body because I was very petite, cute and slim. The fact that I could dance helped my transition a bit easier. My cousin had given me a bathing suit, and I bought me some Payless shoes, the ones with the grandma heels.

By the time I had gotten offstage, the manager said that I needed to buy me some real heels, ones that would make me look sexy and not like a little girl. The club even had people who made clothes for us and sold them. The outfits ranged anywhere from $25 to $150. Don't get me wrong. The outfits were nice, but I couldn't see myself paying that much for an outfit that I was going to be taking off every few minutes.

After working at the black club, I wanted to try the white clubs because you got paid more money. For some reason, the black club had started settling for $5 a dance whereas the white clubs started at $10. I began working at a white club where they served food, and the white men loved small petite black girls, so I fit right in. The white club had what you called the mother who supplied your makeup, wipes, feminine products, etc.

She even helped you get ready to go onstage. Ms. Bee is what we called her. She was about 66 at the time and loved smoking her cigarettes. Of course, you had to tip her every night as well. The funny thing was that Ms. Bee would love to help you with your makeup.

No offense but this was a lady who was old, wrinkled and reminded me of Tammy Faye with all that makeup. Now, how was she supposed to make me look good when she was a hot mess herself?

The bouncer at the club was huge; I'm talking about over six foot tall. One of the girls who worked with us was over six foot tall, and everybody thought she was a man, but everyone in her family, even her mom looked like that because of the country they were from. Her name was Blair, and we immediately became friends.

A lot of the girls were afraid of her because of her size. Well, even Blair was in for a surprise because the club had Wednesday night women's wrestling and she was the champion. I am 5'2" and at that time, I only weighed about 100 lbs.

I grew up wrestling and fighting, but there was a trick to winning the wrestling match. To make it interesting for the guys, we had to be covered in whipped cream.

The trick to winning was you had to make sure they didn't put any on your hands or knees because that would make you slip and lose every time. Of course, I couldn't reveal the secret because I got paid to wrestle and what I didn't make on the first shift that made up for it and I went home afterward.

The only thing I hated about this club was there were three stages to dance on and whoever was on the main stage got to pick the music. I've danced to rap, alternative, country, the dreadful dead; you name it, I've listened to it. I met a guy name Daniel and after two weeks of dating, he moved in with me.

Sunday night, a country singer came in. He was very nice and even invited me and a couple more girls back to his place. Of course, Daniel wasn't having that. So I settled for an autograph instead. So many important people had come through this club, doctors, lawyers, basketball players, entertainers; you name it, they were there.

So many women were into plastic surgery.

Blair even had one done. Her boob job was obvious because she didn't have any breasts to begin with and now she had these hard breasts that were like rocks. I remember one afternoon while getting ready to work I looked up, and Blair didn't have but one breast. She looked down and began to cry.

The night before, she and her husband who was like 5'2" were fighting and he pushed her down the stairs. Well, the sack busted and she looked funny for about two months dancing with her hands over her breast until she could afford to have her breast redone.

Maryland was another dancer who had a boob job, but her breasts were fine. She just wanted more. I thought about getting a lift because my breasts hung so low you would have thought I was from Africa. It's a good thing that we had makeup because I would sit and watch Maryland use so much makeup to cover up her stretch marks. Guys really don't know how many alterations these girls had to do to themselves before they came out of the dressing room.

All sorts of stuff started happening at the club. The D.J. would be dating some of the girls and even kissing them inside the booth. One guy would come in and pay Blair $100 just to step on his foot with her heels because he was into pain. Now, why couldn't I get a fool like that?

What I did get was something I didn't ask for. One day I was eating at the bar, and I looked out of the corner of my eyes and the guy sitting next to me was masturbating. They had to throw him out and yes, I lost my appetite.

You had Asian men who only liked the blondes with long hair. I remember patting one on his head, and if looks could kill he would have. I didn't know that they consider that bad luck in their country.

On my 21st birthday, I got paid $100 to drink a shot of tequila. We had this one guy who was a millionaire who would love to play pool with us, and he would pay us $20 a game.

Well, Jack started doing drugs, and we started taking advantage of him. When he wasn't looking, we would put the balls in the hole so we could start another game. I wonder what happened to him afterward.

We had one girl who was on acid and boy did she snap. I remember asking her a question, and she snapped at me, so I just reminded her that no matter how high she was if she ever disrespected me again I would blow her high. Even though I was small, I was feisty. You had to be that way; otherwise, that world would take you over.

The owner of the club had several clubs even in Las Vegas. There had been rumors that a lot of those managers were sleeping with some of the girls, but none of my friends did. However, one of my friends would sleep with some of the guys who came in. She would blame it on the alcohol.

A lot of the girls were paying their way through school, and a lot of them started doing drugs and just fell off. One girl who worked there briefly was very acrobatic and entertaining.

Carmen had served time for killing her husband in self-defense. We would smoke weed before we went to work. One day, Carmen was crying and asked if she could stay with Daniel and me for about a week until she could save up some money and leave town. Sunday was my favorite night to work, so I had my customers let her dance for them, and she made about $700 that night.

I didn't know she had a pimp and that all of his girls stayed with him in bunk beds. She said that every night after she went home he took her money and only gave her $10. After a week, Carmen stayed in a motel and tried to have sex with Daniel. Of course, I didn't find out until about eight years later.

After about a year, I had gotten bored. I had gathered a lot of clients; at the black clubs they don't have to get to know you for you to dance for them. I had gotten bored of the white club because after my fiancé Daniel left me, things just weren't the same because that club is where we met. It held so many memories so I headed back to the black clubs because my confidence had gotten stronger and so had my dancing.

I even had invited a girl name Tamera, who I kind of took under my wings. She had a regular job and was going to school, doing something with her life. The night crowd at the black clubs was totally different from the white clubs. Guys thought they could touch you, and it would be okay. Well, it wasn't okay for me and one time I even slapped a guy because he touched me in the wrong place.

One of the bouncers had a crush on me so he just kindly picked him up and threw him out. I know a lot of you are saying I'm crazy to hit a man. Well, I grew up fighting boys so I knew if I hit one I had to be prepared to fight like one.

I worked at several strip clubs and when I got

tired of one I went to another. Pimps were at an all-time high. I remember one asking me if he could be my pimp. I laughed in his faced and said that I wanted his money, and that wouldn't work for me.

I'm sorry but, I don't need a man telling me how I should spend my money. He's not the one who is taking off his clothes and putting up with all the mess these guys are saying to you.

Everyone knew all the girls who had pimps because they either had a tattoo with their pimp name on them or they had to carry a pouch with their money around their neck. Those girls stuck together. I remember a couple girls got into an argument with some of the pimp girls.

The next thing I knew, that pimp had pulled up in a van and all his girls beat the crap out of those girls.

We even had one lady we called Peaches. At that time, she was in her late 30's, and we called her the madam. Her husband was pimping girls as well. I remember one girl in particular. Her name was bowleg, she had a body that all of us would die for but from the neck up, something went wrong, not only was she cross-eyed but let's just say looks were not a part of what we wanted to have from her.

She ended up getting pregnant by Peaches' husband and things kind of got ugly between them from that point on.

All the managers were married and sleeping with some of the girls. One of the managers was dating one of the girls, and they were in the mall. Well, they ran into his wife, and the girl (China Doll) was left standing there with her mouth open.

China Doll loved to gossip and that caught up with her. She was sitting in a chair in the dressing room when my cousin slapped her out of the chair. She just took that beating. There's no way I'm going to let anyone beat me without putting up a fight.

They wouldn't let me jump in. I didn't need to anyway because my cousin had that on lockdown and I made sure that no one interfered.

My cousin was the one who you really had to make mad before she said something to you. I was just the opposite. I was the type who said it wasn't over unless you were knocked completely out.

My day of fighting didn't come until later on down the road. I was talking to this guy who I really didn't like but because he bought me anything I just went along with it. I even had given him a key. Later, I found out that the girl who he was sleeping with besides me used to be all in my face and was getting ready to go out of town with some of us to Miami to strip.

These were the days when your cell phone was in a briefcase. I started looking at my phone bill, and I started calling back numbers that were on my bill. One of the numbers happened to be one of his baby mamas. After speaking with her, she thought that was me who came to her son's birthday party—it was not.

She and I became friends even to this day. I couldn't wait to get to work that next week. I confronted him and the only thing he said to me was, well, if he hadn't have done it to me I

would have done it to him. I slapped the f---
out of him and told him to give me my key
back.

We were in the VIP room. He started running.
I jumped over my manager who was sitting
right there and this time when I hit him he fell
off the steps. It's a good thing someone was
there to catch him.

I asked the manager what would happen if I
got into a fight with one of the girls. He said I
would get a three-day suspension. I had made
enough money to be out for a couple of days
so, I plotted this thing.

I knew China Doll, the gossiper, would go
back and let her know what day I was coming
to work; well, the trick was on them.

They thought I was coming back to work in
about two days. Well, I came back the next

day. I was well prepared; I had my knife in my bag just in case her sister who was a waitress wanted to get in on the action.

Before the girl got to work her sister pulled me to the side and said that she wouldn't interfere with the fight because her sister had slept with her baby daddy and do whatever I had to do.

I went into the bathroom and when I came out she was sitting in the dressing room getting ready. I could tell she was nervous. I started looking around because I knew I was going to bust her side the face with a chair but I had to be realistic because depending on how hard I hit her with that chair I didn't want to end up in jail either.

All of a sudden, I grabbed the chair and busted her with it against the mirror. I just started beating the crap out of her. The next thing I knew, one of the girls who was about 6'2 swooped me up. Well, in the middle of the swooping the other girl was able to grab my hair, and someone had one of her hands. I was thinking to myself if that girl let's go of her other hand she will sneak a lick in so what did I do next? I pulled a Jeffrey Dahmer on her. I bit down so hard on her breast you would have thought I was eating a piece of chicken. After she let my hair go, that's when I really got her. By that time the manager was in there and they had her in the bathroom. I knew I was getting ready to go home. That's why I didn't bother getting undressed. I pulled out my knife because I was prepared for whomever. After being suspended for a couple of days, I came back to work and the guy was sitting in VIP with (BB) a local comedian. I kindly threw him his clothes. They started joking him out because all his clothes could fit into a Kroger bag. I didn't fight the girl because of jealousy. It was the principle. I will not allow you to sleep with someone I was sleeping with and smile in my face at the same time. She thought by sleeping with him he would buy her things like he did for me. Well, she ended up being the one buying for him. Every night there was always action at the clubs. I remember one night seeing one of the daytime dancers do a whole eight ball of cocaine and pass out. Back then, the only thing I was into besides cigarettes was marijuana because I had to be high to even look at the guys I would dance for.

I know they would wonder why sometimes I would be laughing or as they saw it, looking seductively. Little did they know I really wasn't looking at them. I was just high. There was a truck stop on Rock Creek Highway where the truck drivers would stop in and one night it was slow, and a girl asked if I would take her and a customer to the hotel and wait for them and he would pay me $80.

I had to ask the manager because anytime you leave the club you had to let them know, especially if you were coming back. They were only in the hotel about 15 minutes; then we headed back to the club. Peaches used to take them all the time but she wanted more money, and the guy didn't want to pay what she was asking so I volunteered my service.

There was a lot of jealousy toward me because I made my money the honest way. A lot of girls got more money because they would let the guys play with them or pay them to have sex. I remember one guy said he would pay me $250 to sleep with him, I turned him down, and the other girls said I was crazy and went after him. Some of those guys, one guy in particular, when I first got on the floor, his pants were white, and about 30 minutes later they were dirty where some of those girls had been riding his crouch. Nasty is what I call it.

A lot of us got to do bachelor parties or parties in particular but depending on who the guys asked, some of the girls and their clicks didn't want me to come along because I didn't do what they did.

One party I did I drove my own car because I never knew what kind of crazy people we were dealing with. One time this girl got paid to invite some of us to a party in B-Town.

The girl left, and I had to drive all those girls

in my car. My car was a 1988 Honda Prelude. As we were leaving one of the girls had stolen this guy's 18 karat gold elephant statue. I made her get out of the car and put in by the garage because the guys had left.

I know when that guy got home he must have said all kinds of stuff about us. See, all it took was one girl to give us a bad name.

I got the chance to do a party for a famous football team. I really liked that party because everything was done in a professional manner. They had a charter bus pick us up from the club. We then picked the guys up from a restaurant and headed to the Hilton hotel. Once we arrived, we were paid a fee up-front, and we had to work for our tips. We had steak, lobster, crab legs, alcohol, etc. The food was delicious. After we finished dancing, that's when the extra activities kicked in. Girls and guys went into separate rooms. I stayed with the girl who was gay and when they asked, I said I was gay also. That way, they wouldn't want anything from me.

The other girl and I got so full; we almost ate it all. People were in the bathroom, bedroom, just all over the place. I walked in on one girl who was having sex with one of the players; it was like a show because a lot of us stood around and watched. The problem I had was, this guy wasn't circumcised, and his penis looked nasty. This girl (Candy) was a professional and didn't care who watched. I also did a party for some doctors at a house. They were also professional. I took my roommate along because she was a dancer.

Also, rent was due, and she hadn't been to work all week, laying low at the crib with her boyfriend at the time.

They had invited some other girls from another club. I'm trying to figure out who invited them. We got paid $175 up-front plus tips where they only got paid $75 up-front. These girls were fat and nasty looking.

One girl had on some long white boots with a big safety pin holding up the zipper and missing teeth. I was laughing because these girls were trying to do anything to get more tips like my roommate and me. Well, they were lucky they got $75.

There were times when the police raided the place and took all the girls back in the dressing room. To work at the club, you had to buy a license. I think they were $65 back then; they've gone up now. Some girls weren't even old enough to work at the club so the managers let them out of the back door so they wouldn't get fined. Those same girls got busted down the road when one of their uncles came in the club while she was on stage.

Now, the two girls were smart because they were seniors in high school and they couldn't spend too much of the money because their parents would be wondering where they get that money from.

Some of the guys got a ticket as well. I've been to court twice on charges that the police claimed they saw me do. I went to court and the charges were thrown out because the police had lied on me. I've seen a lot of actors and rappers come in the club. They were very nice. I was even in one rapper's very first video, Player's Ball. I could name a lot of them who came through the club but I won't.

One of the clubs I worked at had this gay lady bouncer named Dana. She was huge and could fight like a man. One night this customer came downstairs because one of the girls had told this guy she would sleep with him so she took his money and ran downstairs. He wanted his money back, but he got his face thrown into the lockers and out the back door. The same girl who did this was known for stealing guys' money like that.

One night, she did it again and ran and jumped into my car and let the seat down. I saw the guys looking around the cars looking for her. My heart was beating because I didn't know what was going to happen. After they left, I told her to never do that again and get the f--- out of my car. Well, she and another girl pulled that on some guys from Miami and days later they found their bodies in the back of a trunk with a bullet in each of their heads and their fingers broken. They say in Miami that's a sign of stealing when they break your fingers. Don't know and wasn't trying to find out. Another girl, Rachel, who was also in her 30's, died. She was always in a good mood. Even when I wasn't, she would smile. She also had money. They say one night she left the club, and they found her car and her body in a lake. They had killed her and duct-taped her feet to some bricks and threw her in the lake. That was a sad moment for me because I didn't get into this line of business to be a victim or a target. I liked stripping because my first year I made over $100,000. Where it is today, I can't even tell you. I blew so much money, giving it away. My advice today is if you are going to be a stripper, invest your money wisely.

Remember Tamera? Well, we fell out because she was living with her boyfriend Melvin at the time who was really a good guy and was cheating on him with a manager from the club who liked me.

I kept wondering why all of a sudden she left her panties in her purse for Melvin to find. It was so they could break up and she could move in with the manager Charles from the club. Charles was cute; he walked with a cain and had a little money and two wives at the time. That's why I never talked to him. But Tamera took that as an opportunity to make her move.

She moved in with Charles, and things got worse for her. She eventually started using cocaine and having wild escapades with Charles and other females. They say years later she moved to South Carolina. Charles went to jail for drugs.

I remember seeing him at Quick Trip off

Pleasantdale Road. I didn't even let him know I saw him. He was a hot mess. I thought he was a homeless man because that's what he was looking like. He had lost everything and was driving a car worse than mine.

I remembered him because of the limp and cain he used to walk with. A lot of people asked me if I was ashamed. For what? I enjoyed the money I was making and if I hadn't worked there I never would have gotten to learn what actually went on at these types of clubs. I'm just happy that I didn't let what was going on in there take me over and have me strung out somewhere.

2

MISCELLANEOUS JOBS

I've worked several jobs in my lifetime. My mom has always said to always have something to fall back on, so I guess that's why I learned many trades. One of the jobs I worked for three years was a door and window company. I really liked this job. What I didn't like was the fact that those people didn't have a backbone. Every time they wanted to know something or wanted to leave early, I would be the one to ask the manager. I was an account executive, which means I dealt with customers and contractors all day long.

I had to watch what I said because one day I thought I had put my phone on mute and I started cursing this guy out, then he starting apologizing. I had to play it off like I was talking to a co-worker. From then on I made sure I unplugged my headset before I said something out of the way to a customer. Only three of us were black; the rest were white. The drama started to unfold between the white women and boy was it funny. It felt good because I was used to working with a lot of black females who kept up the mess. They always assumed I was making a lot of money because they never saw me in the same outfit. As I explained to them, they can have what I have at a fraction of the cost. They were paying wholesale for one pair of jeans, and I could get the same jeans for only $5 used. I just knew how to bargain shop.

One of the girls, Meagan, was blonde and pretty. She decided to get a boob job, which was fine with me. Then her husband got jealous because he paid for them and then she starts tripping. They soon got a divorce, and she started seeing one of our managers who left his wife for her, and they got married. Another girl, Mary, was only 25 at the time and was on her third marriage. I felt sorry for her second husband because he really was a good guy and he was also her manager's son. Mary left her second husband who was a good man for some old ugly who was a piece of shit. We even had one guy who almost got one of my friends fired. He went telling customers that he was gay, and that was wrong so he's lucky he didn't get fired over that. Just because you don't like someone does not give you grounds to talk to customers about them either. But he paid for it. They ended up firing the guy who was talking bad about his co-worker to a customer. You had to be careful when you dig a ditch for somebody. The reason why I left this job was because I was sick of playing Toby. We had about six people helping out answering the phones. David and I answered the most calls. We both averaged about 650 calls a week each. My supervisor Eden who I adored so much, told me that the next day they were going to take everybody off the phones except me and David and put, Carmella and Andrea on the phone. The problem I had with that was that between the two of them they may have done about four hours a day of answering the phones and it wasn't many, which would have left more calls for me and David.

I told Eden I wasn't coming back after that day. He thought I was kidding. I told him that tomorrow if he noticed that I wasn't there, that was my notice. Needless to say, I didn't look back. I walked out on faith. I look back on some of the stupid mistakes I have made while I was using drugs, and I remember working at the cosmetic factory, which I loved, but at the time I was only a temp and when it came time for me to be considered permanent I had to take a drug test, which I passed, but it was so stressful because I had marijuana in my system so I used my two-year-old son's urine at the time. I put it in a Ziploc bag and held it between my thighs the whole ride there because it was during the summer and it was scorching hot. I lost out on the job because I started telling them about my health problems and then they wanted my medical history and notes from doctors, and then I was out of a job. I had started using cocaine on the weekends with my boyfriend who introduced me to it. The weekend high turned into during the week high. I had a very good job in Alpharetta most people would have killed for. Sometimes, after getting high the night before, I started calling in sick. I loved getting high, but the after effects I couldn't handle. I would be in bed after I came off my high with my head under the covers because my head would be throbbing and it literally felt like someone had run my body over with a bulldozer. I would have nose bleeds off the chain. I had done cocaine so much in one night that my heart started racing, and I couldn't breathe. I went to a doctor; that dumbass said I had a sinus infection. I'm like, you don't see all this caked up powder in my nose? I would have sores in my nose. I would use a bobby pin to get them out, and when they were stuck, I would blow them out of my other nostril; they were the size of a bullet. Cocaine had me chain smoking either cigarettes or black and mild's. I also had to have something to drink because it would have your throat very dry. One job I applied for, it would have started me off with $45,000. I had passed every part of the test, and it was now time to take a drug test. I hadn't smoked marijuana in like three years, so I wasn't worried about that. It had been three months since I last did cocaine. People say that it is out of your system in like three days. Well, the lab called me and said that they found traces of cocaine in my system and did I care to explain? I said no. They forwarded the results to the new job and low and behold I didn't get it. From that day forward I left cocaine alone.

3

THE CLEANERS

The cleaners is a place where my mom works. She has been at this particular job for 20 years. That's a long time to be with a company, and she hasn't missed many days throughout the whole time she's been there.

My mom doesn't take off work unless she's really sick and I mean really sick. On the other hand, I got to play sick at least once every three months.

The only men in this company are the owner and a supervisor. The rest of the cleaners are women. The white women work in the front at the counter, and all the blacks worked in the back on the machines.

No, it's not a prejudiced company. It's just that the owner hasn't found a white woman who can stand to work in the back and have to deal with all the drama that unfolds.

I'm not saying that the white women don't have drama, but you don't hear them arguing and carrying on like the blacks at this job. I've been back home for about three years now, and I know their cycle as if they were on their period.

The summertime is when all the women in the back start to argue and not speak to each other. They start back talking around late October because they want to talk about what all they are going to buy when they get their income tax money. They continue to get along until around march throughout the summertime.

My mom is very light skinned, short, hair cut short, and can really dress. Well, the women in there are so jealous of her it's unreal. I mean, every day they stare her up and down just to see what she has on.

You have some that even try to copy her style, but it won't work. This one lady who works in the same station has already been to prison for killing her cousin so she doesn't mind fighting. She pays about $60 a week for somebody to mess up her hair.

I could have done a better job for half the price, and I don't know how to style hair. The problem is that she is bald headed in the center of her hair, and she would be having like three or four different hairstyles in one. I would be ashamed to say I'm her stylist.

This same lady (Cora) is also related to my sister's mother-in-law (Sue), and they go to the same church. The funny thing is that they don't get along, and Cora and Sue are sitting at church arguing and talking about each other where other people can hear them and then always want to say they are saved. Well, I don't know what kind of saved they are, but I would not want to be going to their kind of church knowing they are caring on the way they are. Cora and my mom have gotten into it several times, but they haven't managed to get into a fight just yet. Robin has been at the cleaners just about the same time frame as my mom. I remember one day my mom came home and said that Robin told her that she couldn't stand her and not to ever speak to her. I asked my mom what she said. She said she just started laughing and implied that was fine with her. That didn't last long. After about two months Robin apologized. My mom said that at least she was honest with her, and she respected her for that. Shonda and Tammy started the feud between my mom and Robin. She fell out with Robin because Robin didn't pick her up one night to go to a party. How petty. Betty teamed up with the two sisters, Shonda and Tammy. Betty is another co-worker who I called the do flunky girl; As long as Shonda and Tammy aren't around, she will speak to my mom, Cora and Robin. They called my mom and the other two the three senior citizens because they are the oldest. A bunch of lonely women if you ask me. Tammy was seeing a married man who is friends with my mom's ex-boyfriend. I noticed that as long as my mom was with him, she thought she could come back to work and say little things that would piss my mom off; I told my mom I couldn't be working there. My mom is a Virgo, very easy going. And I am a Gemini. Everyone knows how blunt we are and don't mind telling people off. Tammy is jealous because her man was married and her stupid self would be taking his wife to the store. I mean, how stupid is that? She even went so far as to try to hook up one of her friends with my mom's ex, just to try to throw up in her face.

Well, my mom had had enough. Finally, she set her straight and let her know she couldn't care less about him and to please refrain from even mentioning his name because she had moved on. My mom did move on, and it was killing them that they didn't know anything about the new man in her life so they decided to try a different route. They started calling my mom's house and playing on the phone.

Shonda even called Robin's mother-in-law house telling her that she only wanted to get back with her son because he had money and that she had AIDS. She even told this 76-year-old lady her name. How stupid was that or she just didn't care. Well, when they got to work the next day, of course, the arguments started back up.

Shonda even called the housing authority and starting making up lies about Robin to try to get her kicked off section eight, but the fool didn't realize that the person on the other end of the phone was Robin's niece so she made the call for nothing then had the audacity to even give her real name. Who the hell does that?

My mom doesn't like to get in any of their mess so she just stands there and starts laughing, which really pisses them off.

Then they had a guy call my mom at work and threaten to kick her butt about some he say she say mess, so now my mom doesn't take personal calls unless we say our name.

They even called my mom's house and told her fiancé at that time not to talk to my mom, and she was only using him to help out with the bills. Now, I'm sorry, but the Bible says that if a man doesn't work he doesn't eat so, in order to live in my house, he has to be helping pay some bills.

My mom got married on her birthday, which was September 14th. That morning someone called my mom's house to try to convince her fiancé not to marry my mom. They acted like this man had money. He worked check to check like I do. It would be different if she was marrying a millionaire.

October 4th, my mom called me to say that

she had gotten into an argument with Shonda and that Shonda was getting ready to slap my mom in the face, but the supervisor grabbed her hand, and Tammy came up and was pulling on my mom's shirt. I asked my mom why she didn't knock the hell out of her. She said the only reason she didn't was because her husband told her not to be fighting at work. "Damn your husband," was what I said. I was mad by now so I called the sheriff to see what she needed to do.

The sheriff advised my mom to come and talk to the judge and if he found reason they could issue a warrant for their arrest because Tammy shouldn't have put her hands on my mom. I called my mom back to see what she was going to do, especially since the owner could care less about the situation. She said she had a headache and would think about it.

By now she's gotten me upset so, I tells her that she's been there 20 years, and there's no way I would let them treat me like I'm nothing and, I would be looking for another job and if she wasn't going to pursue the matter then, do not call me back with the drama and hung up.

I couldn't wait to call and tell my sisters. My mom only called me because she knew I worked out of town and it would take me a minute to get to her job. My sisters worked near my mom. She knew not to call them because all hell would have broken loose and I probably would be bailing all of them out of jail.

My mom finally decided to see what could be done and asked if I could take off. I had already told my boss what was going on so she said I could leave and handle the situation with my mom. After arriving at the sheriff station, they said I needed to go to the courthouse to speak with the judge. The lady at the counter said because my mom didn't call the police when it happened she would need to go to the police station to file a complaint first and if the police couldn't handle it, then come back and at that time she could speak to a judge. I can understand the proper protocol so we headed to the police station. An officer at the police station asked my mom what was going on and after my mom explained she asked us to follow her back to my mom's job.

The owner was nowhere to be found, and she needed to take statements from everybody who witnessed what went on, but they all had left for the day. My mom called the owner to see what time he could come the next day to speak with the officer, and he advised her

7:30 am. Later on that day, the owner called Robin at home and told her not to come to work till 7:00 because by the time she got to work everything would be over. Well, he didn't even show up so the police didn't take statements but said she would be sending him paperwork to fill out and that my mom needed to be documenting every incident from that day forward and save it and if any type of harassment should come up again to call them right away.

Needless to say, the owner is nothing but a punk, wimp, and a coward. He acts like he is scared of those women, but he really didn't care as long as they got his work done.

He shouldn't have two sisters working on the same shift anyway, especially ones that keep up the mess every day. My mom says, so far it's been quiet, and all they have been doing is just looking. Three years later, Cora decided to retire and just draw her social security and came back to help out when people would be out sick or didn't come in that day. Shonda always had a thing for the owner. She would wear these short skirts; I guess trying to entice him, but he didn't pay her any attention. She had started so much drama till he got tired of her and fired her. Tammy then began to start missing days from work until the owner finally had enough of her and she was also fired. That left (Betty) the do flunky all alone with Robin and my mom. Betty no longer had her alliance with her and eventually found herself another job at another cleaner. The women talked about trying to get rid of my mom and Robin for years and in the end, everything that they plotted backfired and now the cleaners is a peaceful place because all the drama and the hell raisers are gone.

4

THE WOOD

I started back working four weeks after I had my daughter and this place beats any soap opera that comes on television today.

First off, the first day I got to work, I knew just about everybody's business. They are good about filling you in on everyone instead of letting you find out on your own.

About three days later this guy was trying to talk to me and the first thing they said was that he was a nice guy who was married and a few months before I came here he found out that his wife was sleeping with someone else and that the child he thought was his was actually the dude she had been seeing.

It turned out that the guy who was trying to talk to me was my daughter's father's cousin, which was great because I don't date people I work with not in this particular field because I can usually guess about what they make anyway.

I was the only black person who worked in the office and the only female who worked upstairs with all these men who thought I would be intimidated by them but little did they know what they had in store. One of the guys (Lucifer), I will explain later why I called him this, was very nice, as a matter of fact, too nice. People, when someone is too nice by all means watch them very closely. People in the plant thought that we were seeing each other because I would always go to lunch with him. He was buying so I would go and listen to some of the stuff he would be talking about. One day on the way back from lunch he assumed that I was making about $6 an hour the same as the guys starting off in the plant. I kindly advised him that I would never drive more than 30 minutes away to any job just to make minimum wage.

If that was the case, I could work in my hometown for that. Albany, Georgia's economy is much different from Atlanta where I was used to making more money because the cost of living was higher. They started me off with $8, which I took for now and till this day I never tell people what I make because it's none of their business.

Anyway, he said that Mike, one of the owner's brothers, is our top salesman and if he calls you are supposed to jump to his every beckon call. Well, I'm sorry, but I told him that if Mike does get smart with me, I will get smart with him as well because I don't let anyone handle me like I'm nobody. He then goes on to say that his wife used to work there, and they fired her. My words to him were that if I come back from lunch and Mr. Cheevers tells me that my services are no longer needed, I wouldn't be mad because just like I found this job, I can get another one.

Finding a job was the least of my concerns. Well, he couldn't just up and go because after talking to him I learned that he was on parole, and he couldn't just leave this job, which is why I guess he puts up with their mess. I later found out that the reason why they fired his wife was because she was the receptionist and every time she answered the phone she was rude. Tracy was another girl who started the same day I did. She handled all the scheduling with the drivers. They say you can tell a lot about someone the first time you meet them, which is mostly true.

While we were filling out our paperwork, I spoke to her, and she just looked at me. Well, I thought she was Mexican and just didn't speak any English. She looked like she was either on crack or some strong medication.

She was much younger than I was with either four or five children and was married. Because I worked upstairs any gossip that pertained to either the people in the plant or downstairs I never knew about until somebody volunteered to share information with me.

Low and behold she had started seeing one of the managers at the plant who was also married. Her husband had jumped on her and beat her up so she moved out and got her own place. A new driver who was about 18 had just started working with us. He was cute, and she seized the moment.

It wasn't the fact that she was 25, but now two men were fighting for her attention. She let the married man go because he was strung out on drugs to the point where he had to go to rehab and quit working altogether. He had been with the company over eight years and you just never know what kind of people you are working with because he hid it all so well and I usually can tell if someone is on drugs having done drugs myself. Tracy and her new man seemed to get along pretty well. After about a month of dating, he moved in with her and her kids. They had even planned to marry, which I knew that wasn't going to happen because as soon as a pretty girl comes along he was going to leave her because Tracy wasn't pretty and you could see that he was just using her for a place to stay and to drive her new Expedition she had just bought.

After the manager had gotten out of rehab, she wanted to spend time with him so she would leave the new guy at home with her sister to watch while she lay with the guy from rehab. It wouldn't surprise me if he slept with her sister because she would leave him all the time with her sister.

Things for Tracy and her young man started to turn for the worst, especially after she gave him gonorrhea. The both of them ended up quitting because they wouldn't come to work. They hired the driver back, but Tracy hasn't been back since.

A lot of the guys in the plant had a tab going where if they borrowed money from the company they had to pay it back, which would be deducted from their check. When my car had broken down, the company paid the bill, and they took the money out of my check until my debt was paid off.

Now, the owner doesn't lend out money because he claims we don't have the money right now. A lot of the guys would be in and out of jail, and the owner with a kind heart would bail them out of jail and, of course, they had to pay him back. Every so often the police will come by with the drug dog to check out the plant to make sure no drugs were on them. If they were to come into the office without telling anyone they were coming and demanded everyone do a drug test. I promise you only six of us would pass. One of those six people (Ramona) is on strong medication so she might test positive. It's hard sometimes to even talk to her because her mind is in a million places. She has about 16 different types of medication that she's on. I would have to be on medication to deal with the way the owner talks to her. He's tried several times to fire her because she messes up all the time, but that wouldn't do him any good because she is best friends with his wife and she would only make him hire her back so he just tolerates her.

Even the managers would have some type of drugs in their system. I've never seen a place where there is so much jealousy among the men. One day I said that I was going to bring them a bag of Depends because they act like babies in here when things don't go their way.

It's like they are in a competition with one another. I called them the office snitches because they are quick to run back and tell what you say but when the flip is switched they get mad when you tell on them.

That's like the pot calling the kettle black.

The reason why I call this one guy Lucifer is because he usually has hell in him most of the time. Lucifer is a Seventh Day Adventist and has what I see as bipolar disease. His wife controls him at home so he thinks he can come to work and take it out on everyone else. We called Fridays freaky Friday because you never know what's going to happen. One incident the receptionist we had at the time was new and very vulnerable. I told her that she needed to stick up for herself and don't let these guys talk to her any kind of way, and I give her three months of hanging around me, and she would have developed a boldness she has never seen before. I don't mind helping people when they asked in the right way. Lucifer had asked me to get something but didn't tell me what he needed and walked off.

He's good about that. A customer had needed to sign a quote, and he failed to tell me that part or else I would have been in a hurry to help him. Well, I heard him say that if these girls would do as I asked them he wouldn't have a problem.

First off, I don't have to do anything for anybody if I don't want to. I was sitting at my desk so I politely yelled out what girls are you talking about because I don't like to get in between other people and their mess.

Darryl, another engineer at the time, also asked who he was referring to. He said I'm talking to the both of yawl. That was my cue then because he had included me in the equation.

I walked out of my office and went right to his desk and said I don't know who you think you're talking to, and you don't intimidate me just because all these men are standing here. Now I don't know what your problem is but if you want me to help you, you need to learn how to talk to people. He then goes on to say he doesn't want to ask me to do anything for him. So I said good and I won't. I also told him that the only thing standing between us was opportunity and air. Now I'm the clerk for them, which means if you piss me off I won't fax or do anything for you. That lasted for about three months of him not speaking to me, which was fine because it got quiet in here. I remember when Daryl and another guy who used to work here that started back working here. He threw a hissy fit at his desk, just throwing things and talking out loud. The problem was he was mad because they just got here and was making more money starting off and he had been here over five years.

One of the positions that the guy had, they

offered to him, but he couldn't handle it, so that's why he's still where he is today—nowhere. Let someone get a new computer and he throws a fit about that to. He's so nerve racking because it doesn't matter if you are talking to someone else he always has to comment by saying here's what I think. Did anybody ask you what you think? He says stuff and the next minute he forgets what he just said. That's why I started documenting what he says because he's not wrapped too tight. One Friday when I came upstairs, everyone was trying to tell me what to do, so I said hold up. Let me go downstairs and ask my boss what's going on because I don't take orders from them. My boss asked me who said that, so I called out everybody's name who had something to say including Lucifer.

I was sitting behind my desk talking to Daryl when Lucifer stood at the doorway, pointed his fingers at me and said why I tried to get him in trouble with Mandy (my boss). I said what are you talking about. He then says shut the hell up and walked away. Okay, by now it's on. I kicked the chair that I was sitting in, back and went after him. When I got to his desk, I looked at his eyes and they were fire red; Satan had crept in. He then jumped his fat ass on his knees to the floor, puts his hands in a cross-like formation and said back up, back up. His voice had gotten deeper. I then said, I'm not going anywhere and that I was going to confront the demon that was inside of him. I said I don't know what your problem is but you're not going to say something to me and expect me not to say anything, and just because your wife at home is not giving you any attention, you're not going to take it out on me. I also said that he was full of hell and matter of fact, go to hell. He then puts his hands over his ears and starts shaking his head saying no, no, no, no, no. By then I'm laughing so I said Lucifer get up off that floor, and he got up. See, if it had been his doing, he could have easily resisted and just stayed on the floor, but because I knew the spirit he was operating in and I was able to call that thing out, Satan had to flee. He gets up and dials Mandy on the phone saying that I was at his desk and wouldn't leave. I said, make me leave, and I'm not going nowhere. By this time Mandy and his boss came up and told him to calm down because I wasn't trying to get anybody in trouble and that she told him that I told her everybody's name who was involved. I then told him, don't you ever walk away from me when I'm talking to you and went back to my desk. I didn't even realize all the other people in there were just standing watching and laughing. I went outside to cool off. Some of the guys said they didn't ever want to get on my bad side, didn't nobody tell him to take that gray reserve tape off my mouth. I get along with everybody here. When everyone else is having a bad day I'm always in a good mood, and I wasn't going to let him spoil it. One guy wishes he had a camcorder because he wanted to send it to America's Funniest Videos. I said was it that good? He said it is the best showdown he's seen since he's been here. After that, Lucifer started throwing stuff on my desk and told Mandy I owed him an apology, and he wasn't speaking to me until I did.

Mandy said I guess you won't be speaking to Each other because I wasn't going to apologize and he didn't even apologize to her when he tried to go off on her. His problem is he doesn't like taking authority from women for one thing. The office was quiet for the rest of the day, but they were making fun of him.

He even had the nerve to tell Daryl that the only reason why he jumped on the floor was to keep from knocking the hell out of me. Daryl told him I'm sorry to tell you, but I think she would have knocked you out, which he was right because I was already in a fighting formation and was ready to fight.

I would have slapped him through that floor and thought nothing of it.

Chad is one of the owner's brothers who also works here. Over the years, he's taken a lot of drugs and is sickly now. He's always walking around here saying he's got about two more years to live, which is irritating because I told him to stop always relying on what man says and what did God say and that if he believed that he only had two years to live he probably was going to die if he kept manifesting it.

People don't realize that your tongue could help or hurt you depending on what comes out so you have to be very careful what and how you say things. Well, it wasn't long before he and Lucifer started to bump heads. Some people you can't give authority to because they will lose their d--- mind. Anyway, Lucifer walks over to Chad's desk and throws some paper at him and says just fixed the d--- thing and that he was his boss and shut the hell up. Chad is somewhat like me; the only difference is sometimes you can't get him to shut up once he starts talking about the same thing over and over. I've learned to just walk off when he keeps repeating himself. Anyway, Chad snapped. He said you aren't my boss, you're nobody, and if he opened his mouth up again he was going to beat the hell out of him.

Lucifer wasn't his boss. He just was responsible for checking over Chad's work to make sure it was correct.

When one of the managers would come into my office, he would always be sniffing, and he stayed congested. In my mind, I knew he was snorting cocaine.

Well, it had gotten so bad that one day when I got to worked I noticed he wasn't here.

He had checked himself into rehab for 30 days because he was about to lose his family. He was married to the owner's sister, so he was in the family and had been here over 18 years. It's good to have a company that will let you get yourself together instead of just firing you. I don't know if they would have let me stayed till I came out of rehab.

He had been hanging out with Ken, another brother of the owners who was a lost cause. He had about seven kids; one was in the same grade with my son. He always looked a mess when he came to work and I thought my ironing was bad. He was always wrinkled and never came back to work on time on Fridays after lunch. That's because he and the manager would be getting high and I know they were getting the good stuff because the manager was getting about $6000 a month.

Mr. Cheevers ended up firing Ken (his own brother), and he went downhill from there. Mr. Cheevers children, on the other hand, were out of control trying to compete for his attention. Joseph, the baby, is all messed up. I'm constantly praying for him. Since I've been here, he's been in a motorcycle accident where he broke his back and legs and has pins embedded in him. Several DUIs, including one in Florida where his father had to bail him out. He seems to destroy everything he gets. He bought an Explorer from one place, which was nothing but junk because he had to end up trading it for another truck.

Well, we all had bets on how long he would keep it clean and not tear it up. I won the bet. It only lasted about a week before the side mirror on the car got ripped halfway off. Joseph really is a good worker when his mind is on it.

When he's not working, you can always find him sleeping at his desk. One day, Daryl took a picture of him sitting at his dad's desk taking a nap and put it on the company website. The reason why it was hard for Joseph to stay awake was because he had stayed out drinking, doing drugs the night before and came to work to sleep. If he had been at anybody else's job, he would have been fired. He's only 19 and been working with the company since he was like 14. He says he's going to college next year. I sure hope so. One Friday while Joseph was at lunch, his dope dealer came up here because Joseph had owed him about $200 and he wasn't leaving till he got it. (Chad), Joseph's uncle, had to run him off. That was so embarrassing to have your dealer come on your job and rat you out like that. Joseph had got tired of this place, and it was taking a toll on him because you could see it on his face. He started his own pressure washer business and was doing well. I hated the fact that some of his family members would say negative things like he'll be back and he doesn't know what he's doing.

At least he stepped out on faith and was trying. I could tell he was happy because he looked different with a glow.

It wasn't long till he got arrested for speeding and evading an officer, let alone driving under the influence with drugs in the car. His dad took his car, and he just went ballistic. He started a fight with his brother Ralph after work and their sister Tina who is a cry baby did what she does best, cry.

Chad and some other guys had to break up the fight between them. He ended up going to rehab for a while and had to come back to work here to help pay off his debt.

When Mr. Cheevers wasn't here, his children

tried to act like they were in charge but as soon as something goes wrong, they are quick to leave you there hanging for you to get yelled at.

I pray daily before I come to work because I never want to get into it with Mr. Cheevers. They act like they are scared to go into his office when he is yelling at other people, and what do I do? Just walked right in, in the midst and he calms down.

Being the owner of this company, there's nothing that gets past him including when we are goofing off on the internet. I admit I used to stay on it a lot, but it really is for my business outside. My computer got a virus on it, so now I only go on to check my emails.

Sometimes, I do play around when I don't have a lot of work to do like now. I decided to write this book on company time and not at home because writing this book at work is really therapeutic and enjoyable because I can laugh while I'm writing and people here are just wondering what the hell I'm laughing at.

There are a lot of people like me just goofing around at work, but let me make it clear, I goof around when I don't have enough work to do and to make time pass by since the internet for me is being monitored, as if I really care.

Every time they turn around they want to have a meeting. I'm glad that I don't have to go to any unless I'm really asked to. Last year Lucifer cost the company over $150,000 because of all the errors he kept making, and now the company won't pay us.

Well, because of that we only got a 50 cent raise. The year before that I got a $1.75 raise, which brought me up to $10.00. Now I'm making $10.50 an hour, and the economy is still going up. He says that we are broke, and we can't get a good raise right now.

The only reason why we even got 50 cents was because everyone started to complain that if we're not making any money why would you go ahead and hire a new sales manager.

We had another receptionist who is so country until it is unreal. Everybody who calls me asked who is that answering the phones and how country she is. It took about a month before we really started talking and I schooled her quickly not to let these guys intimidate her, and she did a good job keeping them in line. My little protégé. I really should have taken psychology because I was giving advice on a constant basis throughout the day. She was a train waiting for an accident.

That poor girl had more problems at a young

age; she just turned 21 this year and reminds me of one of my sisters who love drama. She loves dating older men, which isn't a problem except she like dating married men.

Yes, I dated a couple of married men in my past but I've learned from my experiences. That's why I'm able to let her know it's not worth it and to walk away.

The receptionist was the type of person who felt like she had to lie and tell you what she thought you wanted to hear instead of the truth.

That didn't work with me because I could read right through her lies and confronted her every time. She would always let her family and friends dictate her life instead of making her own mistakes.

That's a part of learning. She was so full of

pride, which made me remember how prideful I used to be. I prayed a lot for that girl because as I got to know her, she was in a sense like a little sister who I grew to actually like. She is very smart but, is throwing her life away. I told her to go back to college; she has no children or a husband holding her back. She's very good with computers and putting things together. It made me feel good when she told me that she was really listening to my advice even when I didn't think she was. Part of her problem is that she longs for someone to really love her, and there's nothing wrong with that except, she is so used to having a man in her life until she feels so empty when she doesn't have a man even if it means causing her to be unstable.

Every day she would come to me about some married man who would just keep calling her until frankly I got tired of telling her the same thing over and over again.

Finally, I just said look just stopped answering your phone. Better, yet change your number. This girl would talk over 3000 minutes a month on her cell phone. She has that phone glued to her ears from the time she came to work until the time she went to sleep. Ain't that much talking in the world.

She reminded me of my sister who always told lies until she forgot who all she told her lies to. My thing is if you're going to lie, at least tell the same lie to everybody so you won't look so stupid.

I'm truly convinced some people are not happy unless they are arguing or fighting with someone 24/7.

Even though I don't say anything, you can't put anything past me because I have this instant radar that knows when something isn't right. I even know when someone has been in my office and even on my computer. It's this vibe I get when I walk into my office.

I know these people think I'm crazy because I'm forever anointing my door and things with oil (olive oil). I know some of you were just wondering what kind of oil it was. Hope that answered your assumption.

She had an affair with one of the salesmen, who she thought I didn't know about but later confessed to, but my radar had already gone off when one Friday at work she asked him to take her home to take a dryer she had purchased back to the store. Well, she only lived up the road, and it shouldn't have taken that long. I guess she thought no one would put two and two together.

She even had an affair with another co-worker who is married, which I sometimes just quiver when I look at him because he is cute but that don't mean as a man he can control his hormones because if he could, he would have never cheated on his wife. Sometimes I wonder why but I guess she and his wife had something in common, like their size. He doesn't know that I know, but I do. Even though he sometimes flirts with me, it doesn't bother me because I don't even look at married men like that, and I never let it get out of hand. If he says something that I think is inappropriate I just won't answer him back. Then he knows he's crossed the line.

I could have easily had a lot of these guys on harassment charges, but I'm not that kind of person because deep down they really are intimidated by me and I guess I'm their little fantasy they will never have. You know the saying, once you go black you'll never go back.

The manager who they hired for the salesmen, he and Lucifer, sometimes I wonder if they eat from the same table or each other's ass because that's what their breath smells like.

The only other thing is that Lucifer's body sometimes smells like that to. At first, I thought it was because he smoked cigarettes but that's not the case. A lot of guys here smoke, and a couple of them chew and dip snuff/tobacco, and I've never smelled their breath or body before. The scent is so bad till I just close my eyes and back my chair up because one of them loves to lean over my desk and talk to me. I've said in a polite way that I don't like cigarette smell and to back up. What I should have said was, your breath stank and please go see a dentist because that's not normal for a smell like that to be coming out of your mouth.

I gave him a break and didn't say that, but I sure did want to. They ought to be glad I've changed for the better because the Old me wouldn't care about hurting your feelings.

Lucifer knows a lot about computers till I think he has found a way to tap into the system. We have instant messaging on our system where we can talk to one another at work and if we are on the phone that's a way to send a message to let us know what they might need.

One day, he had his shirt unbuttoned where you could see his nappy hair chest. As a man, they should always have on some type of t-shirt underneath because maybe it's just me, but it makes a man look sexier and attractive to look at and not just some hair bulging out at you.

Well, anyway, the receptionist and I started texting each other about it. The next day, he came into my office and asked me why was it a deal about his shirt so I asked how did he know. Okay here was the bomber. He said that he was at home, and the message came across his computer. How were you able to get a message at home that wasn't sent to you? I told my manager. So Mr. Cheevers had to go with another program where if it's tapped into this time your computer will fry.

He still knows how to get around these systems because he wanted a report from me one time and I told him I didn't have it on my system. He then says that J.D. could do it from his computer but probably wouldn't and all I have to do was put in Mandy's password to get in, but I didn't hear it from him.

What you just did was confirm what I have

been saying all along. Don't trust him because you never know what all he could tap into.

The only reason why they haven't let him go is because they really can't afford to pay someone else what they're really worth to do his job so they just tolerate him and talk to him any kind of way.

If these people were working in corporate America, they would have been fired a long time ago with no hesitation.

Ralph is the oldest of Mr. Cheevers' children who really doesn't know what direction he wants to go. Mr. Cheevers wants to retire and let his children take over the company, but that would be a big mistake because they would run this company into the ground.

Since I've been here, I noticed that he doesn't like to really work, and he and his other brother and sister like to throw temper tantrums. If they get into an argument with their dad, they get mad and storm out of the office for the rest of the day. Now, if I storm out, that would just be my job.

He hates to admit when he messes up and will leave you hanging. I remember one time when their father wasn't here they messed up and instead of staying in their father's office to hear him fussing, they left Mandy in there to take the blame and then later came to her and apologized.

Such cowards. Poor Tina, if her dad even gets loud with her she starts to cry and leaves for the rest of the day. She also wants to be in control but doesn't know what the h--- she's doing. She went to medical school but works here with us. She really wants Mandy's job, but she really couldn't handle it.

I wouldn't want Mandy's job either even though I could do it, I just don't want to have to be around Mr. Cheevers unless I really had to. Nothing against him it's just that I see the way he yells at everybody and one of two things would happen with us.

One, I would be fired for sure but not without giving this man a heart attack because I'm sorry, but I don't care if you do sign my paycheck you will not talk to me any kind of way and, you will respect me just as I respect you. Come to find out, I make more than Tina does. She ought to be glad she has the kind of dad she does.

He pays for her new truck, the insurance and the daycare for her child. That doesn't stop these spoiled children from being so ungrateful.

Ralph decided that he would tell the guys

what quote for them to do and he also was in charge of checking their work. Well, we have a problem because he sometimes leaves and doesn't come back and no one knows he's gone.

He and his brother would sometimes be standing outside for 30 minutes at a time. I've never seen people here take so many cigarette breaks. Mike called one day and was pissed because Ralph wasn't here to check behind the guys work and he didn't have his quote to bid on. That's his nephew. What did he expect me to do? Things go in and out of people's ears around here. Anyway, the next day when he came to work, his dad got onto him. When I got ready to walk into my office, I noticed some quotes were left at the edge of the door on the floor.

I asked who put them there. Chad said that

Ralph had put them there. I politely walked over to him and said they will just sit on the floor because I wasn't a dog, and he could have left them on my desk like he usually does.

I was waiting for him to say something to me. He then calls me into his office and asked me why I didn't let him know that we had a job that bid and no one checked it over.

This was my opportunity to really tell him off. So, I just simply said that I couldn't tell you if something was due if it was closed out of the system and hadn't been checked over.

When I was passing out quotes to the guys, I never closed it out until I actually had it on my desk. What he would do was he would check it complete when the guys put it on his desk, but he didn't actually look it over yet and would let them sit on his desk for a couple of days.

Once something is closed out of the system, you can't actually look and see what's due for that day unless you actually do a search and at that time, who wanted to because had he followed protocol we wouldn't be having this problem.

He didn't say anything to me then. The next day he said he would just let me start back handling the quotes again. He should have done that in the first place, and that was another way of him getting out of work.

I just pray that these children grow up. I was looking for a quote that was due, and I couldn't find it, I told Ralph about it, and he asked me why didn't I put who I gave them to. I said first of all I didn't know I had to pick up behind grown men, and I didn't mind doing it but let me know. Don't just assume

I'm going to do anything. He runs his a-- downstairs to complain to Mandy as if I wasn't doing my job. Mandy calls back upstairs, so I went downstairs to let her know that the problem had been solved.

By now Tina calls me because Mr. Cheevers thought that I was upset.

I'm not upset. I said, I don't like for people to Ask me to do something and don't give me time to try and fix the problem, and these were a bunch of men who needed to grow up and stop running back telling everything they heard.

Tina said we would have a meeting on that Monday. Well, that morning Ralph found the quote and plans that I was looking for Friday rolled up on his desk in another set of plans. So, basically, the meeting was about something that he lost and didn't even acknowledge that he had made a mistake.

What he did was quickly say that he and I had come to and understanding, so that I wouldn't let everyone know he had f---ed up. They also said that the guys took too many smoke breaks and assigned them times they could take one.

The next day that was broken as if they could care less. We now have a new receptionist who is about 22 with three kids. Once again, someone decided to let me know that she is living with her kid's father whom she's been with for nine years who she is not married to.

Now that's dumb on her part. Anyway, Joseph starts liking her to the point where every time you look up he's at her desk.

One day she took him to court and was gone a long time; it doesn't surprise me if they detoured to his house and had a quickie. He got mad because someone mentioned that he stayed at her desk too much. Now the same married guy who slept with the last receptionist is hanging around her desk also.

It's funny because they act like little children around here. Joseph is a good worker if he applies himself. Otherwise, he's a bomb waiting to explode. That child got issues for days and demons by the minute.

On Fridays, one of the reports that I do has the amount and dollar amount of quotes that each one does. Well, I would let them come to my desk to look at the sheet. Well, this particular Friday I decided to post outside where they sit. Okay, now he got really mad and said that the report was only for his brother and dad to look at. What did I do?

I pushed him out of the way and took it down and said anybody could get the report if they wanted it and it's mighty funny that as long as you are the one who is leading with the most money you brag and boast about it, but as soon as someone else beats you, you start whining and get mad. I then went on to say that from now on if he wanted to know what he did to go to his brother and don't ask me anymore. Afterward, it got so quiet till you could have heard a pin drop. Joseph had the nerve about two weeks later to sit at my desk and say that he's going to testify at church, so I asked him what he was going to testify about. He said about drinking and doing drugs. So I asked if he still did those things, and he said yes. So by now he's getting ready to really get it from me. I told him that he couldn't testify to something you haven't overcome yet and that God would be judging him. He then asks what is he supposed to tell those young men, and I said nothing because they would consider him a hypocrite because what if they saw him at a liquor store or even in his own home? How would that look, especially with your father being in the church and all?

But then again, his father raises so much hell at work until he doesn't count either. He just built the church but has someone else preaching in it. He even had the nerve to tell his uncle that he wished he was dead.

While he was sitting at my desk was my opportunity to give him some advice. I did tell him that he was dead wrong for saying that to his uncle and when all else fails to just pray for his uncle because I would have never told anyone I wished they were dead. He was mad because Chad had mentioned that he was growing drugs out of his house, so I said, sometimes the truth hurts and that two wrongs don't make a right. Just forgive him and move on.

I'm not saying forget but just move on. Scott, the sales manager, one day at a meeting tried to blame something on me to cover his own self, but I didn't even get mad. I just starting laughing because sometimes you really just have to turn the other cheek. Until this day, I didn't even let him know I know that he lied on me. You can kill people with kindness. It doesn't matter if you're black, white, female or male, drama is still drama. Coming from the corporate field into a small business where all the family members worked here made me realize that there is more to life than just this job and my destiny is not tied up in this place.

I've enjoyed working here, and this place holds fun memories that I will never forget but working here for the rest of my life just isn't me. Going from paycheck to paycheck just isn't cutting it.

I'm tired of borrowing money from loan companies and sick of them calling my job.

One time they called and asked for me, so I said she's not here. Can I take a message? One lady asked me my name so I said, Selena. She then said no you're not. By then I'm pissed and said you cannot tell me who I am and I would take a message for Sharon to call you back. She then asked for my supervisor so I put her on hold and hung up.

My supervisor would have just told them I can't take personal calls. Another time a man called and so the receptionist told him I was gone for the day.

He then goes on to ask her how long I had been gone so she says, she doesn't know, and who was calling. He then goes on to say he was a friend so she says, I'm her best friend, and she tells me everything.

By then I picked up the phone to listen to see if I recognized his voice. He then says that I was supposed to be picking him up and that he was waiting for me, so she says well, give me your number and I will have her call you back. He then says he's calling from a pay phone. I guess he thought that would get me to the phone. He got to wake up a little early to try and get one over on me.

I told her to tell him to hang up the pay phone and stick his head out. She should be coming around the corner soon. The games that these loan companies play just to try to get you to the phone.

And for what? I can't pay you if I don't have the money and why do they always call during the week, every day? Don't they know most people get paid on Fridays so if by Monday you don't receive a payment, what makes you think you will get a payment on any other day?

After saying all of this, people, if you are unhappy with where you are in your job, maybe it's time for a change.

You can either choose to make something happen or continue working for people who make things happen. As for me, I'm going to continuing praying and asking God to place me where my destiny lies, which is not in this place.

Best wishes.

Sharon

CPSIA information can be obtained at www.ICGtesting.com
Printed in the USA
LVOW11s0736280816

502109LV00001B/8/P